Puerto Rican Patriot

The Life of Luis Muñoz Rivera

Puerto Rican Patriot

The Life of Luis Muñoz Rivera

By Mack Reynolds

Illustrations by Arthur Shilstone

Crowell-Collier Press ⚭ Collier-Macmillan Limited ⚭ London

To Former Governor Luis Muñoz Marín of Puerto Rico

LIKE FATHER—LIKE SON

Contents

Puerto Rican Patriot

The Life of Luis Muñoz Rivera

Introduction

For some reason the truly outstanding men of the world—especially those rewarded with titles such as "father of his country" or "George Washington of his country" or "national hero"—are usually thought of as men coming from great countries.

Such men are George Washington, first president of the United States; Julius Caesar, founder of the Roman Empire; Alexander the Great, conqueror of the ancient world; Peter the Great, the most pro-ressive czar of Russia; Charlemagne, emperor of Western Empire; Alfred the Great and Richard ion-Hearted, rulers of England.

reatness of a national hero, however, should

not be measured by the size of the country of his birth. It must be measured by the depth of his understanding and the extent of his accomplishments for his people. Thus it is that a man such as William of Orange, who liberated the tiny Netherlands from mighty Spain and became the first king of modern Holland, was as great a man, perhaps, as the Mongol conqueror Genghis Khan, whose empire once spread over half the civilized world.

Perhaps William of Orange was even greater than Genghis Khan. The famous Mongol was a man of destruction; where his armies passed there was often no living thing left behind. But William of Orange was the founder of what is now one of the most prosperous and happy lands in Europe.

What of the really tiny countries? Can their national heroes be ranked alongside the great rulers of world-wide empires?

Can the national hero of an island such as Puerto Rico, only one hundred miles long by thirty-five miles wide, one-third smaller than the state of Connecticut, with a present population of less than two and a half million, be rated with the truly outstanding leaders of the world? This will be shown.

Most Americans know very little about Puerto Rico. Indeed, for the first thirty-two years of the

United States' possession of this Caribbean island, between 1900 and 1932, the name of the island was not even spelled correctly by most Americans. Even in official U.S. Government documents, maps and geographies, its name was misspelled as Porto Rico. However, considering its size, Puerto Rico has had possibly more adventure and romance concentrated within its area than any equal-size territory that is part of the United States.

It has had explorers such as Columbus and Ponce de León. It has had pirates such as Sir Francis Drake and Sir John Hawkins (although they didn't call themselves pirates, but privateers). It has had Indian massacres and desperate men who fought for gold. It has had war and revolution; unfortunately, more than its share. It has had rich times—very, very rich times—when the galleons of Spain, transporting the wealth of Mexico and Peru to the Old World, swung at anchor in Puerto Rican ports. And it has had desperately poor times when hundreds of thousands of its citizens had to flee from the island to the mainland in hopes of finding work there.

This story of Luis Muñoz Rivera, national hero, will begin then with a thorough look at the land of his birth—Puerto Rico.

1

The Coming of the Spanish Conquistadors

The first white man who ever saw Puerto Rico was a sailor on Christopher Columbus's flagship. The man was probably on watch when the landfall, as sailors call it, was made. Undoubtedly he yelled, "*¡Adelante! ¡Tierra!*" (Ahead! Land!), and shortly afterward Admiral Christopher Columbus came out of his cabin to look.

The admiral's real name was actually not Christopher Columbus, and he probably was never called that in his entire life. He was born in Genoa, Italy, and was christened Cristoforo Colombo. He sailed, of course, under the flag of Spain, and there they called him Cristóbal Colón, as he is still known in Spanish-speaking countries such as Puerto Rico.

Columbus had a dream of sailing west to find the fabled East Indies. He spent many years trying to convince first the king of Portugal and then Ferdinand and Isabella, the king and queen of Spain, to supply him with the ships and men needed for the adventure.

The sighting of what is now Puerto Rico took place on November 19, 1493, one year after Columbus's history-making first voyage with the *Santa Maria,* the *Pinta* and the *Niña.* On that first journey, the *Santa Maria* had a crew of only fifty-two men, and the other two ships were manned by only eighteen men apiece.

When Columbus made his second trip, his flagship, which he had sentimentally also dubbed the *Santa Maria*, was at least double the size of its namesake. And he had sixteen other ships to accompany him. Among them was the *Niña,* which was not only a veteran of the first voyage but was also later to participate in the third journey in 1498. Under Columbus's command that tiny vessel sailed altogether more than 25,000 miles, the equal of going all the way around the world.

On his first voyage, Columbus had reached San Salvador, a speck in the Bahamas now called Watling Island. On this second voyage, he was exploring farther south in the Caribbean, and discovered various other islands besides Puerto Rico, including the Virgin Islands, the Leeward Islands, St. Kitts and Jamaica.

In fact, he approached Puerto Rico from what are now called the Virgin Islands, and which are now possessions of the United States. He left the largest, St. Thomas, and headed almost due west. Puerto Rico lies only about forty miles from the Virgin Islands, so there was no difficulty in navigating—one island can be seen from the other on a clear day.

Nevertheless, these were strange waters, and it was necessary to proceed slowly for fear of submerged reefs and rocks. To be safe, on the night of November 18 the men dropped anchor off the small island of Vieques, part of the Puerto Rican island group that also includes tiny Mona and Culebra.

In the morning, there was Puerto Rico, an island the Indians called Buriquen, Boriquen or Burenquen. Columbus promptly changed this name to San Juan Bautista (Saint John the Baptist) in honor of a saint regarded with great respect in Genoa.

However, for a time the men didn't land; the winds were so favorable that it would have been a shame not to take advantage of them. Instead, they spent all day of November 19 sailing along the beautiful southern coast of Puerto Rico, outside the line of dangerous reefs.

Most of the Spaniards on that voyage estimated Puerto Rico to be about the size of Sicily, an Italian island in the Mediterranean Sea. Actually, Puerto Rico is only about one-third the size of Sicily. The only person to have a more accurate idea of the size of Puerto Rico was Doctor Diego Álvarez Chanca, a physician from Seville, Spain, who had come along with various other passengers. He estimated the island to be about thirty leagues long, and since a league is about three miles he was approximately correct.

That night the fleet rounded Cape Rojo, the southwestern tip of Puerto Rico. The men lowered sail once more for the night, for safety. In the morning they raised sail again and entered into what is now Boqueron Bay, an excellent harbor.

Some of their supplies were running low, so two days were spent gathering water and whatever else was easily obtainable, including wild grapes. Passengers and crew not needed for other duties went fishing, since fresh fish were always a welcome change from the provisions carried by Spanish ships in that age.

Others hiked inland and came across a deserted

village, which had about a dozen huts built around a plaza. One house was much larger than the others and had roofs woven with leaves and twigs. The men compared the village to the garden arbors in Valencia, Spain, where some of the men had lived. For some reason, they supposed that this small settlement was a summer resort town of the Carib Indians.

They found no Indians to trade with, because the natives had fled to the hills as soon as they had seen the white men.

The truth was, these inhabitants of Puerto Rico were not Caribs. And it is probable that Columbus's expedition was just as well off that they weren't, because the Caribs were not only cannibals but some of the fiercest fighters that the Spanish were ever to encounter in the Americas. Had these been Carib Indians they most surely would have put up a fight and attempted to repulse the first landing of the white men on Puerto Rico.

The Indians who vanished into the hills were members of the Arawak stock, a gentle people who had originated on the mainland of South America and crossed over to the islands, possibly as recently as only a hundred years before Columbus's fleet arrived. They were a small race, less than medium in height, and practiced agriculture, at least on some of the islands. They were advanced enough to make pottery. Different tribes had spread over the islands as far as the Bahamas, where Columbus had first contacted them when he landed in San Salvador.

These, then, were the early inhabitants of Puerto Rico. It was estimated, later, that the island held at least thirty thousand Arawaks. In less than a century there would not be one Arawak remaining alive. They made poor warriors, and they made even worse slaves. Between the raiding Caribs and the grasping Spanish colonists, they failed to survive.

At daybreak on November 22 the fleet raised anchor and left behind it the newly discovered Puerto Rico. The expedition headed for the larger island of Hispaniola, upon which the modern nations of Haiti and the Dominican Republic are established. Columbus had discovered Hispaniola on his first exploration trip.

Columbus returned to Puerto Rico the following year. He evidently was still under the impression that the island was inhabited by Caribs. By this time his fleet had run afoul of these cannibals on several occasions and had had some pitched battles with the fierce warriors. He was planning to return to Spain and wanted to capture several Caribs to take back to exhibit to Ferdinand and Isabella. If he could not capture any Caribs on Puerto Rico, he intended to sail farther south to where he had originally come in contact with them.

Sailing down from Hispaniola, the fleet pulled in at little Mona Island, just off the southern coast of Puerto Rico proper. It is still called by the name that Columbus had given it. The Spanish sailors of the expedition who kept accounts of the trip described the island as being about eighteen miles around and rich with a fertile yellow soil in which very large manioc roots grew in abundance. Cassava is made from manioc roots and is still used in Puerto Rico for its food value, various dishes being prepared from it, including tapioca.

The admiral, however, was foiled in his plans to raid the natives. Even as his fleet began to cross the narrow passage from Mona to Puerto Rico, he fell seriously ill with a high fever, and then became delirious and went into a coma. He had been pushing himself too hard in his explorations, and lack of sleep and the poor nourishment had caused his illness.

His captains and other ranking officers held a meeting and decided to abandon the raid and return north. So once again the gentle Arawak Indians of Puerto Rico were temporarily spared their eventual fate.

Although Columbus was finally cured, he never saw Puerto Rico again. The island was later settled by survivors of his disastrous fourth voyage. He had started that trip with four caravels and possibly one hundred and fifty men, returning to Spain in September 1504, with only one of the small ships and with his son and brother and twenty-two others. The remaining survivors chose to remain on Hispaniola. Later, many of them helped to conquer Puerto Rico, under Ponce de León, and became the island's first settlers.

The story now turns to a remarkable man who has a two-fold position in the history of the United States. Juan Ponce de León was not only the conqueror and first governor of Puerto Rico but the discoverer of Florida and the first white man to explore any of the territory that is now the United States. He did the exploring for a rather unusual reason.

Probably no two men have had more effect on Puerto Rico than Juan Ponce de León and Luis Muñoz Rivera. However, two men could hardly have been more different, for one was a man of war and conquest while the other was a poet and a hero of peace.

Juan Ponce de León was born in 1460 in San

Servos, which was part of the Spanish kingdom of León. He came from an old aristocratic family but was not the eldest son and therefore did not inherit the family fortune. Like other second sons in Spain, he had to seek out his own livelihood. At the time, the wars between the Christians and the Moslem Moors were taking place for possession of Spain, and the young Juan Ponce de León joined the forces of King Ferdinand and Queen Isabella.

He fought with distinction at the conquest of Granada, the last important battle that drove the Moors from Spain. But then the war was over, and like many Spanish men-at-arms he found himself without employment.

Also like many other Spanish soldiers, he became excited by the prospect of conquering new lands when the word came through that Columbus had discovered islands in the Atlantic by traveling west. He decided to join Columbus on the second expedition to the Americas.

So Juan Ponce de León was with the fleet when it first saw Puerto Rico in November of 1493. We can only guess what he thought when his eyes fell upon the island that was to be his destiny.

He did not return with Columbus to Spain at the end of that exploratory voyage but instead stayed on with other colonists in Hispaniola and took serv-

ice under Nicolás de Ovando, who had been appointed governor of the island. From 1502 to 1504 he fought to help conquer Higuey, the eastern part of Hispaniola, and was made governor of that province.

Ponce de León was very ambitious. He wanted an island all of his own, not just one province. He sought permission to conquer San Juan Bautista (Puerto Rico) after the word had spread that gold was to be found there. In the year 1508 the king's permission was received, and Ponce de León set out on the first expedition under his own command. His force of fifty men was to fight an island population estimated to be between 30,000 and 600,000 Indians.

Surprisingly, he had few difficulties. The Arawaks were far from a warrior-like people, and their simple weapons (something like spears) were not even tipped with flint, let alone iron. After a small skirmish, most of the terrified Arawaks disappeared into the mountains and had to be hunted down by the Spaniards, who wished to enslave them and put them to work finding gold. In 1508 Ponce de León founded Puerto Rico's first city, Caparra, located on what is now San Juan Bay.

From 1509 to 1512, he was governor of San Juan Bautista, and he made himself rich in gold, slaves and land. He changed Caparra's name, in 1511, to Ciudad de Puerto Rico. Translated into English that would mean City of the Rich Port, and at that time it was a rich port indeed, since the gold was coming down out of the hills in great quantities.

Other things were happening in Puerto Rico besides the mining of gold. In 1515 sugarcane was brought from Santo Domingo and planted, and in 1518 the first Negro slaves were brought to help in the labor. It had turned out that the Arawaks made poor slaves, and they were often beaten to death when they failed to submit to the crushing work.

By this time, Ponce de León was over fifty years of age. The science of medicine was not yet very advanced, and few people ever reached the half-century mark. He was beginning to feel his years, as well as the aches and pains of the many wounds he had taken in his campaigns.

At this time he began to hear rumors from the natives about a wonderful, rich land called Bimini, which lay to the north of Cuba. But more exciting than the richness of Bimini was an intriguing tale that the island was the location of the fabled Fountain of Youth, or *Fons Juventutis* as it was called in Europe. Supposedly, anybody who bathed in this magical fountain regained his health and even his youth.

Ponce de León applied to the king and received

permission to explore and take possession of this "island" in the name of Spain. And on March 3, 1513, with three caravels, he set sail.

He sailed northwest through the Bahamas, sighted Florida late in March and landed not far north of the present city of St. Augustine early in April. Since the discovery took place at the time of the Easter feast, which the Spanish call Pascua Florida, he named the land La Florida. He then turned south and explored the coast all the way down to Key West and up the west coast to Cape Romano.

Ponce de León returned to Puerto Rico in September 1513, without having discovered the Fountain of Youth. During his absence, there had been a revolt on his island, and he had to take the time to put it down. When the troubles were over, he set sail for Spain in September 1514 and obtained a commission from the king to subdue the Carib Indians and also to conquer and colonize La Florida.

He did not have much luck against the tough Carib Indians, and he returned to Puerto Rico, where he resided until 1521, troubled with the healing of still more wounds. By this time Ponce de León was in his sixties. The Fountain of Youth story sounded better and better to him.

So that year, with two hundred men, two ships,

fifty horses and other farm animals and a considerable amount of farm implements, he set sail again for the island of his dreams.

He landed on the west coast of Florida, probably near what is now Tampa, and made a few trips inland. However, he was continually attacked by the Indians. Always in the front during a battle, despite his age, Ponce de León was finally wounded several times with arrows.

His friends immediately rushed him back to Cuba in hopes of getting medical aid, but the old conquistador died there. Shortly after, his body was returned to Puerto Rico to the San José Church, which is today the oldest Christian place of worship in the Americas. His body remained there for three and a half centuries before it was transferred to its present resting place in the cathedral.

His family coat of arms still hangs beneath the ceiling of the old church, and nowadays there is a bronze statue of him in the plaza. His name comes down to us as the founder of Puerto Rico, the land that centuries later was to become the home of Luis Muñoz Rivera, hero of peace.

2

Indians, Pirates and Wars

Christopher Columbus, the discoverer of Puerto Rico, and Juan Ponce de León, its conqueror and first governor, had now passed away. But a great deal of history was yet to unravel before the birth of Luis Muñoz Rivera in the year 1859.

At about that time, a rather strange thing happened. It will be recalled that Columbus had named the island San Juan Bautista and that its principal town was called Ciudad de Puerto Rico. This original settlement was moved in the year 1519 to its present location, and somehow the names got switched. The city came to be called San Juan, and the island was named Puerto Rico. Nobody seems to know why.

The Indian troubles continued.

When Ponce de León's force of fifty men had first landed, it was estimated that the Boriqueno tribe of the Arawaks numbered anywhere from 30,000 to 600,000 people. They lived in clans, each of which democratically elected a chief, called the *cacique,* who lived in a larger house than the others. This house contained the *zemi,* or idol of the clan. In a way, the house combined the chief's palace and the clan church. Because of the fine climate and the lush soil, the Arawaks had little work to do to provide themselves with a living suitable to the tropics. It came as a shock to them when the Spanish took over and put them to hard labor, panning for gold in the mountain streams.

In 1511 the Arawaks revolted and attempted to drive the Spanish from the island. However, they could not withstand the steel weapons, the gunpowder and the armor of the invaders and were slaughtered in great numbers.

The weapons of the Spanish were not the only thing that finished off the poor Arawaks. The Europeans also brought ills commonly found in Europe. Smallpox and measles, among others, were unknown in Puerto Rico, and the Indians died by the thousands when exposed to these diseases.

There were no members of the Boriqueno tribe left by 1582, only seventy-four years after Ponce de León's expedition had landed. Their place in the hunt for gold was to be taken by the thousands of Negroes brought from Africa on slave ships.

The peaceful Arawaks were not the only Indian people inhabiting the area now called the Caribbean. The name of that sea in which Puerto Rico lies comes down to us from the word "Carib," which probably meant "strange." The word was applied to the cannibalistic, warlike tribes of Indians that were coming up out of South America in their canoes to raid both the Arawaks and the newly arrived Europeans.

Although cannibals, the Caribs were no more backward than the other Indians of that vicinity. In fact, they were in some respects more advanced, their basketwork being highly developed. They were also one of the few people in the New World to have invented sails, which they used to power their forty-foot sea-going canoes. They also had more advanced weapons than the Arawaks, using bows and arrows against their enemies.

Evidently they were a taller race than the Arawaks and sometimes had curly hair, which is very rare among the American Indians. And they were always warlike. They never came to peace with the Spanish.

Year after year, in the dark of night, their long war canoes would slip into Puerto Rico's many fine harbors, and the Caribs, highly painted but refraining from war-whoops or other noisy customs of Indians in battle, would sneak out to attack the homes and settlements of the Spanish colonists. The farm houses or the smaller towns would go up in flames, and by the time the desperate troops from the forts arrived, they would find that the colonists had been killed and that the raiders had made off with all the property they desired.

The original name of the Caribs had been Calinago or Calino. It was Columbus who had changed it to Caribales (or Carib), and strangely enough it is the origin of the English word "cannibal."

The Spanish made little progress against them and it wasn't until other European settlers began to colonize the Caribbean area in the seventeenth century that the Caribs were all but exterminated. A small tribe remained on the island of St. Vincent and mingled there with Negro slaves who had escaped from a shipwreck in 1675. This group was shipped away by the British in 1795 to an island off the coast of Honduras. From there some of them moved north and are located today in Guatemala. A few Caribs also can be found on a reservation in Dominica, one of the Windward Islands of the West Indies, but for all real purposes the race is gone.

Indians were not the only trouble that the colonists of Puerto Rico faced. The inhabitants of other Spanish colonies attempted many times to take over the source of so much gold. As far back as the governorship of Ponce de León, Diego Columbus, son of the admiral, had sent a lieutenant to try to take control. The attempt failed, but many other groups of invaders tried to take over the island. Thus, as far back as that, the politics of Puerto Rico were confused.

Puerto Rico is not a large island, and although the deposits of gold were comparatively rich, they were far from inexhaustible and began to run out. By 1570, the Spanish had taken more than four million dollars' worth of the precious metal from the mountain streams and the mines. Exploration for gold had become less and less profitable.

Long before this, however, many of the Spanish who had settled on the island had become impatient. They had not found the great fortunes they had hoped for, and they began to look for further adventures.

The story now turns to what was happening on the other islands of the area and upon the mainland. Puerto Rico's history is so involved with these places that a clear understanding of Puerto Rico would be impossible without some background on Cuba, Hispaniola, Mexico and Central America.

Although Columbus discovered the islands in 1492, and even cruised along the mainland of Central America in 1503, during his last voyage, the Spanish who lived in Puerto Rico, Cuba and Hispaniola had no idea of the existence of Mexico. One would have thought that having come this far in their attempts to reach China and the East Indies, they would not have stopped.

Nevertheless, it wasn't until November 18, 1518, that an expedition of any size was sent out by Governor Diego Velázquez of Cuba to check upon the tales and rumors about great lands a little to the west and to explore and trade. His force was not meant to conquer the new areas.

The expedition was under the command of Hernando Cortés, possibly one of the most ruthless, cunning and ambitious men in all history. It consisted of eleven ships, 508 soldiers, one hundred sailors, sixteen horses, fourteen small cannon and thirteen arquebuses, similar to shotguns. A few of the soldiers and sailors had been recruited from the dissatisfied inhabitants of Puerto Rico.

From the beginning, Cortés had obviously decided to throw off the command of Governor Velázquez and take over the whole expedition for his own ambitious plans. And that is exactly what he did.

Within two years he had overthrown the Aztec power and had begun to drain Mexico of its gold and silver. As Cortés once told Montezuma, when the Aztec war chief asked why the white men were so anxious for the precious metal, "We Spaniards have an illness, the only cure for which is gold."

After the conquest of Mexico the imaginations of the Spanish became so inflamed that, in both the New World and in Spain itself, a dozen new expeditions started off in all directions to find new kingdoms to conquer, new sources of gold and silver.

The most successful of these was that of Francisco Pizarro, who had accompanied various other ventures, such as that of Balboa, the discoverer of the Pacific. Pizarro had heard rumors of a kingdom of gold on the west coast of South America, and after several expeditions he finally conquered the Incas of Peru.

Peru was even wealthier than Mexico, and the problem became how to get the gold and silver back to Spain. It was too much of a trip to sail around South America, so the only answer was to ship the booty up to Panama, which is the narrowest part of Central America, and then put it all on muleback, where it could be carried across to the other side and then put on new ships to take it the last lap of the journey to Spain.

Puerto Rico was a very convenient stopping-off port for ships going from Panama to Europe, and the island boomed as a result of the large amount of trade with the Spanish galleons.

However, a new problem arose. The Spanish had cruelly robbed and enslaved the Indians to seize all this wealth. Now others, just as cruel, were willing and anxious to rob them. There has probably been no place in the world, no period of history, that saw so much piracy as then took place in Puerto Rico.

Buccaneers from half a dozen European countries sailed eagerly to the part of the Caribbean Sea called the Spanish Main. They came in single ships; they came in fleets. They came in numbers as great as those of small armies, commanded by such desperadoes as Henry Morgan, who in his time sacked many a Spanish city.

Henry Morgan passed close to Puerto Rico many times but never attempted to capture San Juan. The reason, undoubtedly, was that the Spanish had realized the value of the port and had strongly fortified it.

They were forced to do this after the first really strong raid took place by a French fleet. In 1528 the French landed and attacked the town of San German, which was at that time the second most important city on the island. The French were finally driven off but not until after they had burned the town.

So many pirates were in the vicinity that the Spanish government saw that it was either a matter of abandoning the island or fortifying it. In 1533 the construction of the fort La Fortaleza was commenced. However, the location was bad, and it was never finished. The fort was later made into a governor's palace, and has been so occupied ever since.

The highest point at the entry to the harbor was then chosen, and El Morro Castle was constructed there. It was built so well that even today it could probably be defended—against an enemy armed with the weapons of the sixteenth century. El Morro covers more than two hundred acres and was captured only once in its entire history, by the Earl of Cumberland leading an English fleet. He came in from the land side with his soldiers, overwhelmed the defenses and held the town for five months. However, the dreaded plague broke out, and he was forced to return home.

San Cristóbal, an even stronger fort, was also constructed on the Atlantic side of the city, and a wall was erected around the whole town. Two sides of this still remain.

The local citizens must have finally settled back and murmured to themselves the Spanish equivalent of "Now let them come!"

Among the raiders who did come were pirate ships, individual privateers (ships given legal permission by their governments to raid), and entire fleets of English, French and Dutch ships, when those nations were at war with Spain.

They did not have much luck, however.

Fort Morro had its first serious fight with an enemy when the English captain, Christopher Newport, chased a Spanish frigate into the harbor and then freed and sailed off with an English ship that had been captured earlier.

Now was to come the high point in Puerto Rican military history, for on November 22, 1595, a fleet headed by Sir Francis Drake and Sir John Hawkins, two of the greatest naval heroes of England, sailed in toward El Morro. These were the men who had been foremost in conquering the famous Spanish Armada when that great fleet had tried to overwhelm England.

They fought for days and finally Hawkins, the "father of the British navy," was wounded and died. Drake retreated and shortly afterward died of a disease and was buried at sea. The British fleet had been crushed.

But the Puerto Ricans had little time to build new

forts and repair Fort Morro before the Dutch arrived under Bouduwijn Hendriks on September 25, 1625. He had a fleet of seventeen ships and a thousand fighting men. They entered the harbor, captured the city and burned La Fortaleza. They lay siege to El Morro and threatened to completely destroy the governor's troops unless they surrendered. But on November 1 the Dutch were finally forced to withdraw, leaving behind four ships and some four hundred dead.

San Juan was a thorn in the side of any power that wished to control the Caribbean, and in 1776, when Spain sided with the Americans in the Revolutionary War, plans were made in London to conquer Puerto Rico. However, the Caribbean island was too strongly fortified.

So the British tried land-trading. In 1704 they had captured Gibraltar on the southern tip of Spain. Now, in 1781, they offered to trade the "Rock" for Puerto Rico. Spain wanted Gibraltar back, but not at that price. She offered Santo Domingo instead, but England would not trade.

In 1796 there was war between Spain and England once again, and Sir Ralph Abercromby arrived at San Juan the following year with sixty ships, carrying about six hundred cannon. But after two weeks of useless attack, he had to withdraw.

It was the last attack on Puerto Rico until the Americans came in 1898.

In the early part of the nineteenth century the Spanish empire began to fall apart. During the Napoleonic Wars, the Latin American countries revolted and declared their independence. By the middle of the century only Cuba and Puerto Rico still remained in Spanish hands.

It is not that they, too, wouldn't have desired their freedom, but Cuba and Puerto Rico were merely small islands and in no position to fight for it. Spain was still a world power, even though weakened, and attempts to gain freedom were harshly stopped.

The gold was all but completely gone from the mountain streams and the mines. The Spanish treasure galleons came no more to the port of San Juan. The island began to teem with people, and there were few mines or other natural resources upon which to base a living for all.

The people became some of the poorest in all the Western Hemisphere. It was time indeed for some basic changes. A liberator of Puerto Rico was desperately needed by the middle of the nineteenth century.

The man who was to become his nation's

liberator was born in the small town of Barranquitas in the Puerto Rican district of the same name.
The exact date was July 17, 1859. His name was
Luis Muñoz Rivera, and he was eventually to be
hailed as the George Washington of his country.

At the time, his parents could hardly have fore-
seen the future of their son, for they were not proud
people and though relatively well-to-do were not
of the aristocracy. They were educated, religious and
had a great love for their country and its culture—
but to be the parents and grandparents of the two
greatest men their island has produced would hardly
have seemed possible to them on that July day of
1859.

3

A National Hero Is Born

It must have been an occasion for celebration in the home of Don Luis Ramón Muñoz Barrios and Doña Monserrate Rivera Vazquez, for it was their first child.

Puerto Rico is a happy land. Above all, it is a land of music. In those days, when Luis was born, almost everyone played one musical instrument or the other. On such an occasion as this, friends, neighbors and relatives were on hand to celebrate. Everywhere could be heard the playing of guitars, violins and castanets, as well as *güiros* (instruments made from gourds, which are shaken to accompany dances and songs).

Undoubtedly, at least one *décima* was composed, for *décimas* are a very popular type of folk song made up on the spot immediately following some event. If there is a hurricane, for instance, a dozen people the next day have made up *décimas* telling about it. If somebody falls in love or is married, his friends will compose a light-hearted *décima* to describe the event. Any excuse at all will do, for *décimas* are a Puerto Rican institution and perhaps one of the reasons that the island turns out so many poets—their training begins very early.

Needless to say, the proud Don Luis gave a banquet for those who came to the celebration. There certainly must have been *lechón asado*, which is a small suckling pig roasted over an open fire on a spit. Even today the Puerto Ricans serve it on all special occasions, and open stands that sell *lechón asado* are as common on the island as hamburger restaurants are on the United States mainland.

In the way of a special treat, there must also have been drinks such as *horchata*, made of almonds, as well as fruit drinks made from papaya, passion fruit and fresh pineapple.

It was a happy occasion, the celebration of the birth of Luis Muñoz Rivera.

At this point in the story it is necessary to explain the Spanish way of naming a child. In Spanish countries a child's name comes from his father's family name and his mother's. For instance, if the father's name is Muñoz Barrios and the mother's name is Rivera Vazquez, the child's name will be Muñoz Rivera.

Luis Muñoz Rivera came from old Spanish stock on both sides of the family. Muñoz, Barrios, Rivera and Vasquez are all names commonly found throughout Latin America, from the Rio Grande to Argentina. They are not quite as common as Smith or Brown in the United States, but they are very widely known, and the history of all Latin American countries is well laced with them. For instance, Justo Barrios was one of the early presidents of Guatemala; Fructuoso Rivera, the first president of Uruguay; and José de Rivera, one of the outstanding novelists of Colombia.

One of the new child's grandfathers had won fame and various medals as a Spanish soldier. Born in 1797 in Villota del Duque, in Palencia, Spain, he had fought in Venezuela against the South American hero, Simón Bolívar. Following the wars he came to Puerto Rico and became mayor of the town of Cidras.

Barranquitas, the town where Luis was born, is

located in the Cordillera Central Mountains of Puerto Rico. It is almost in the exact center of the island and is only about twenty miles from Cerro de Punta, which, at 4,389 feet, is the highest peak in Puerto Rico.

Barranquitas was and still is a small town. The last official count gives it a population of only 4,268 persons, and it was even smaller when Luis Muñoz Rivera was a boy. Today, as well as then, it is a typical Puerto Rican mountain town. The highest structure is the wooden church with its sheet-iron roof. Public buildings were few and included only two small schoolhouses, both of them inadequate for anyone with the hunger for knowledge that young Luis displayed. Village life centered around the plaza, as in all Spanish towns great and small.

The house in which Luis was born is moderately large by Barranquitas standards, built of wood and with a zinc roof. When Luis Muñoz Rivera died in 1916, one of his closest friends, Don Eduardo Giogetti, bought it and donated it to the Puerto Rican people as a shrine of their national hero. Today it has been turned into a library and museum for all to visit.

Indeed, all Barranquitas seems to be a national monument to Luis Muñoz Rivera. He is buried in the cemetery there, and his tomb contains a small

museum that includes many of his personal belong-
ings, documents pertaining to his political career,
copies of newspapers he edited and clippings of his
poems and articles. His death mask is also there,
made immediately after he died. On the walls of the
tomb are striking murals illustrating his career and
the high points of his fight for Puerto Rican liberty.
The mural was painted by the great Puerto Rican
artist, Rafael Ríos Rey.

But what was life like for young Luis when he
was a boy?

At the time of his birth—more than a hundred
years ago—Abraham Lincoln was about to be
elected President of the United States, and the next
year the terrible Civil War was to break out and not
to end until 1865. On the American frontiers, the
Sioux, Cheyenne and Apache Indians were still re-
resisting the ever-constant thrust of the white man,
who was destroying the Indians' buffalo herds and
plowing up the hunting grounds.

In those days Americans most certainly thought
of themselves as free. However, slavery still existed
in the United States. Also, only white *men* were allowed to vote. Not until 1920 did the 19th Amend-
ment to the Constitution allow women the ballot.

Compared to Puerto Ricans, however, Americans
of 1859 were free indeed. Since the days of Ponce

de León the little island had been under the thumb of Spain.

Not until late in the nineteenth century were Puerto Ricans allowed to have newspapers. They had not even been allowed to have cultural societies to study mathematics, philosophy and the arts, to say nothing of being able to form political organizations.

There was not a single institution of higher learning on the island when Luis was born. Well-to-do families made a practice of sending their children back to Spain if they wanted a university education. A few were sent to the United States, but so strongly did Spain dominate her colonies that when the patriot and friend of Muñoz, Dr. José Celso Barbosa, studied medicine at the University of Michigan and graduated first in his class, the authorities in San Juan would not admit that he was a real doctor. He hadn't taken his education in Europe!

More than 85 per cent of all Puerto Ricans never attended school at all, not even grammar school. They were not able to read or write, and this situation continued until modern times.

An indication of how poor the schools were is to be found in the fact that by the time Luis was ten, he had learned everything that was taught at the local school in Barranquitas, and he then had to study under tutors in his father's home.

Luckily the Muñoz family was fairly prosperous, and his father had a large library. Luis was able to study not only in Spanish but in French as well. His mother had given him his first lessons when he was only four.

Luis was always first in his class. In addition to his regular subjects, he studied music with Don Jorge Colombani. Luis also developed the habit of copying words from the Spanish Royal Academy Dictionary in order to enrich his vocabulary.

Later in life it was Luis' desire to go to Spain to study law, but his father wanted him to go into business and taught him bookkeeping so that he would be able to take over the family's affairs. His father was a merchant, a landowner and the town's notary public. He had once even been mayor.

No one is now alive who played with Luis Muñoz Rivera as a boy, but there are various oldsters around Barranquitas whose parents or grandparents did, for the old families still remain. The tales that come down are perhaps hazed by the long years in between. Some of the stories are similar to those told about George Washington chopping down the cherry tree, or possibly like the story of the young Lincoln trudging miles from the store where he worked in order to pay back to a customer a few pennies that he had short-changed him by mistake.

We are told that from the earliest days young Luis was a leader, a boy with original and inspiring ideas. He did not become the leader of his friends because he was a better fighter or because he was a bully. He simply had better ideas about how to spend play time. They were Arawaks, they were pirates, they were explorers, they were seekers of gold.

Indeed, Barranquitas was well situated for boyhood. Nearby in the hills were Indian caves that existed before the arrival of the Spanish. These caves had paintings on the walls, as well as bits of pottery, broken tools, weapons and other relics strewn about.

In the streams, there were still small amounts of gold, and the boys could play at washing it, though indeed it was so scarce that a good amount of work was required to find even the tiniest amount.

Some of the mountain streams of Puerto Rico seem to vanish in places where there is much underground drainage. Often a river will disappear into a chasm and reappear some distance away. However, the streams are many, and as a lad Luis had numerous opportunities for swimming and fishing.

In those days, life in Puerto Rico was indeed different from what it is today. There were no television sets, no movies, no radios, no record players. Adults and children had to create their own entertainment.

Life was not colorless or uneventful, however. Fiestas, fairs, saints' days and national holidays were considerably more numerous in the countries settled by the Spanish than in North America. And the Puerto Ricans are a gay, laughing, singing people, always ready for a celebration.

It is easy to picture young Luis on his saint's day. In the morning there would be *alboradas,* the songs Puerto Ricans sing in the early morning to celebrate the yearly event that is more important to a lad of Spanish descent than his birthday. Presents would be received from friends and relatives, and, of course, there would be a great feast.

The average North American would probably not recognize a single dish spread out before Luis on a feast day. There would be *arroz con pollo,* which is a Puerto Rican version of a Spanish favorite based on rice and chicken. Or *arroz gallego,* which is diced beef steak with mushrooms, fried eggs, onion, olives and beans soaked up in a yellow-colored Spanish rice. And *asopao,* chicken or seafood cooked with rice and covered with peas, asparagus, pimentos and hard-boiled eggs, similar to stew.

In the evening, after feasting and singing all day, the people enjoy the *seis*, which are folk dances shared by young and old alike.

Luis' days were not all spent at play and festivities, however. From the very beginning he was a serious, intense student with dreams for both his own future and that of his country.

The subjects Luis was taught might seem strange compared to those studied in the United States. And it is probable that of all the great authors young Luis read, only one would be familiar to a young North American student. That author was Miguel de Cervantes, who wrote *Don Quixote,* the famous novel about the last of the knights who went forth with Sancho Panza to tilt with windmills and go through other fantastic adventures. Cervantes was a favorite of young Luis and, for that matter, the older Luis as well. It is said that Luis Muñoz Rivera read the story over and over again.

What other authors did Luis study? While North American students studied the plays of Shakespeare, young Luis studied the works of Lope de Vega Carpio and Tirso de Molina. Instead of reading the verses of poets such as Robert Burns, Wordsworth, Tennyson and Longfellow, young Luis thrilled to the poetry of Luis de Góngora y Argote and Fernando de Herrera.

While students here study the lives of Washington and his generals, Luis pored over the battles of Simón Bolívar and José de San Martín, who between them had liberated almost all of South America from the Spanish in the early part of the nineteenth century. Nor was Luis unfamiliar with the lives of Ignacio Allende and the priest Miguel Hidalgo, who had held high the banner of independence in Mexico and gave their lives for its freedom from Spain.

These early studies of Luis Muñoz Rivera were to be an important influence later in his life when, with all good will perhaps, the United States was trying to impose its culture on Puerto Rico. This fight of Puerto Rico to maintain its own cultural traditions, its own Spanish background, was to be one of the greatest burdens Luis Muñoz Rivera was to bear.

When young Luis was only twelve years of age, tragedy struck. His mother, the gentle Doña Monserrate, had been in ill health for some time. Even in those days, Puerto Ricans were noted for their large families. Luis was the first born, and in the next twelve years Doña Monserrate had nine more boys. It was a drain on her health beyond her frail body's strength. She died, leaving young Luis, not yet in his teens, to be his father's sole aid in raising the family.

Luis took on the job of tutoring the younger boys,

since the local schools were simply not good enough to supply a decent education.

By the time he was fourteen, he was helping his father in the family store and also doing such clerical work as copying legal documents. At fourteen, Luis Muñoz Rivera was in many respects already a grown man, with an adult's responsibilities.

Even as early as this, Luis was aware of politics and the strong currents that were spreading across Puerto Rico. When the Latin American nations, from Mexico to the very tip of South America, had thrown off the Spanish colonial yoke, Puerto Rico and Cuba alone remained in the Spanish king's possession.

Not that they hadn't both revolted over and over again. But for revolutionists such as Bolívar and San Martín to fight against Spanish soldiers in the mountains and wilderness of South America was much different from defying mighty Spain while on a small island such as Puerto Rico. If the patriots met temporary defeat on the island, there was no place to retreat and regroup their forces.

Luis was only nine years of age when the last armed rising against Spain had taken place. In 1868 thousands of Puerto Ricans took up arms in what was called "El Grito de Lares" (The Outcry at Lares). But, as always before, the attempt failed, and in only three days the Spanish authorities suppressed the patriots and arrested and imprisoned or shot the leaders.

This event was perhaps an important lesson for young Luis, even at that early age. In his future struggles for independence against Spain, and later against the United States, he always called for peaceful means to achieve Puerto Rico's ends.

During these years Luis spent many hours seated quietly in one of the town's coffee shops or in the living room of the Muñoz home, listening to his father and the other better-educated men of Barranquitas as they argued the issues of the day.

Luis listened carefully to both sides. Although his father was a Conservative, his favorite uncle, Vincente Muñoz Barrios, was a Liberal, as were a good many other citizens of Barranquitas. It must have come as a shock to the older Muñoz when his son finally decided to join one of the parties and chose the Liberals rather than following in his father's footsteps.

To put it very simply, the Conservatives wished to remain under the Spanish wing, although they wanted Puerto Rico to have more say in its own governing. The Liberals went further and wished to have autonomy, that is, they wished to rule themselves, although they too at this time wished to remain a part of Spain.

In the past, ever since the days of Ponce de León,

the island had been ruled by a series of governors —142, in all. They were usually military men, and always Spanish, never Puerto Rican. Their word was law in military matters and in practically all other community affairs. The executive, legislative and judicial functions of the government were in the hands of the captain general. Offices held by native Puerto Ricans were largely routine; all important decisions were made by the Spanish.

However, in 1870, Spain went through a temporary upheaval, and a liberal government came to power. Puerto Rico was made a province of Spain and allowed to send eleven delegates to the Spanish Cortes (the highest Spanish legislature). Four of the delegates were Liberals, led by Román Baldorioty de Castro, the founder of that party, and seven were Conservatives.

One thing at least was accomplished during this period. Slavery, which had been a curse of the island since Ponce de León's day, was abolished in 1873, almost exactly ten years after Abraham Lincoln had issued the Emancipation Proclamation. Luis was only fourteen at the time, but he was to remember the day down through the years, always considering it the first big step toward Puerto Rico's complete freedom.

In actuality, the Muñoz family had owned several slaves themselves, but Luis' father had always been against the institution and had been in favor of abolishing slavery even without payment to the owners.

Spain was not long to enjoy her breath of freedom and new liberalism. The Cortes had declared the country to be a republic, but that government was soon overthrown, and King Alfonso XII was restored. All the liberal measures that Puerto Rico had hailed so joyously were cancelled, and once again the island of Puerto Rico became no more than a colony.

General Sanz was sent to be the new governor and immediately took steps to throw all the Liberals out of office and to replace them with the Conservatives. He also closed down all the Liberal newspapers and did not hesitate to jail the more vocal of that party's leaders. The Provincial Assembly, which had been so happily hailed by the Puerto Rican people, was simply abolished.

Unfortunately, the island was once again back where it had started.

All this did not pass unnoticed by the young Luis Muñoz Rivera. He continued to study politics and to listen carefully to the opinions of his elders. It was true that Puerto Rican freedom had been given a great setback, but the Liberals were not at all of the opinion that the final word had been said.

Already young Luis had begun what was to be his lifelong profession. He was writing.

Unlike many a beginning writer, he did not attempt to rush into print with his earliest efforts. In fact, he was twenty-three years of age when he first published his stirring poem "¡Adelante!" (Forward!) in 1882. It was accepted by editor Mario Braschi of *El Pueblo*, a newspaper published in the city of Ponce.

Mario Braschi was possibly the first to realize that a new poet of major importance had been found. He immediately urged Luis to follow up his first endeavor with more writing. He also realized that this young man was a potential patriot who could stir the multitude with his verse.

So Braschi wrote to Luis, urging the new poet to devote his efforts to moving men toward science, liberty and betterment, rather than writing love poems, as most Puerto Rican poets were doing.

Luis could not have agreed more. His writing was to be directed toward self-government for Puerto Rico—not toward attracting the romantic sighs of the señoritas.

And in the very next year, 1883, he took the biggest step of his life. He joined the Barranquitas branch of the Liberal party and took a stand he was to hold for the rest of his life: freedom for Puerto Rico!

4

More Toil and Trouble

Joining the Liberal party was not a small step for Luis. It is easy enough in the United States today to become a Republican or a Democrat when most people are Republicans or Democrats and everyone is free to vote as he pleases. But it is another thing, indeed, to be a Washington, a Jefferson or a Benjamin Franklin and stand up against a tyrant who dominates one's country and demand a new type of government.

Luis Muñoz Rivera, though only twenty-four at the time, was destined to become the George Washington of Puerto Rico. In those early days, certainly, his father, his relatives and the neighbors with whom he had grown up in Barranquitas must never have dreamed it.

Luis was to spend the balance of his years in his fight for Puerto Rican home rule, but he, too, could hardly have known it at that time. He still thought in terms of following in his father's footsteps as a merchant and businessman. In 1884 he and a boyhood friend, Quintín Negrón Sanjurjo, went into business as Muñoz y Negrón and opened a store.

The business didn't particularly prosper, since Luis, at least, spent more of his time in politics than he did in commerce. However, he remained in Barranquitas until June 10, 1890.

He soon came to dominate the Liberal Committee in his home town and became its president and also a member of the municipal council. In 1885 he was proposed as a candidate for the Provincial Assembly for the district of Juana Díaz, but the Liberals were small in number at that time and he wasn't elected.

It was in 1885 that he began to come into his own as a writer. He began to place his works in three different publications, *La Revista de Puerto Rico* (The Magazine of Puerto Rico), *El Clamor del Pueblo* (The Clamor of the People) and the newspaper *El Pueblo*.

In 1887 the situation began to heat up once

again. In January of that year the Liberals held a convention in the town of Coamo to reorganize and found a new, stronger party. The convention was a turning point in the life of the still-young Luis, for he met a man who was to influence him possibly more than any other, Román Baldorioty de Castro, the "grand old man" of the Liberal party.

From the beginning, Baldorioty realized the strength of Muñoz and took him under his wing, calling him his disciple. Together with other aggressive young Puerto Ricans, such as the poet José de Diego and Dr. José Celso Barbosa, he planned their new organization, which was called the Autonomist party.

Its new program was simple enough. There was only one thing the Autonomists wanted—home rule. They did not want complete freedom from Spain but only to govern themselves in accordance with the local needs of their island.

It must not be thought that political life in Puerto Rico consisted merely of writing stirring poems for the newspapers and in giving speeches to crowds of *jíbaros,* the simple country people of the island. There could often be much excitement, and in the shifting situation, a man who might be a friend and ally one day might be a rival and even an enemy the next.

The Autonomist party began to grow rapidly, and, needless to say, the Conservatives who backed the new Governor Palacio became afraid that Baldorioty and his group would win out. Harsh measures were carried out against the Liberals. Once again the newspapers for which Luis wrote were closed down, and many of the editors were thrown into El Morro's jail. Some were tortured and beaten.

Ramón Marín, who was later to become Luis Muñoz Rivera's father-in-law, was editor of *El Pueblo*. He shut down his newspaper rather than print retractions, or withdrawals, of accusations against the Conservatives. Francisco Cepeda Taborcias, editor of *La Revista de Puerto Rico*, was beaten up and jailed. The job of editing the newspaper was offered to Luis, and he accepted. But the threats against Cepeda were increased, and he was told he might be shot unless his publication was discontinued.

It was this same Francisco Cepeda Taborcias who became one of Luis Muñoz Rivera's greatest foes shortly afterward. Cepeda took a stand against the policies of Baldorioty, and as a result the old man, who was now ill, was removed as the party's head.

Luis was indignant. It was not the first time that Cepeda had stepped on his toes and advocated measures Muñoz considered to be against the interests of Puerto Rico. Indeed, the rumors went around that Luis' rival was continually making cutting remarks about him. If Luis allowed this to continue he would soon lose the respect of his fellow members of the party. It was finally too much.

Luis Muñoz Rivera had come to his feet quietly. By this time in life he was a tall, heavy-set man, and because of his appearance and bravery was already being called "the lion" by both friends and foes.

At a meeting when both men were present, Luis publicly challenged Cepeda to a duel. Silence fell over the hall in which the meeting was taking place.

Luis then turned and asked two of his friends to act as his "seconds." The two men looked at him numbly, but the *code duelo* (the correct manner that regulated dueling) was most strict in those days and a matter of great formality. Both accepted.

Luis turned and strode from the hall, his face rigid and his head held high.

His two friends approached the surprised Francisco Cepeda Taborcias and asked him to choose his weapons, as well as the time and place for the duel.

Cepeda, still shocked at the challenge, muttered his answer.

The meeting was breaking up into small groups,

and everyone was chattering about the duel. Paco and Eduardo, Luis' seconds, hurried after their friend and overtook him outside. They tried to persuade him not to go through with the duel.

Luis Muñoz Rivera told them flatly, however, that there was no cause he would rather die for than Puerto Rican freedom, and that Francisco Cepeda Taborcias stood in the way of that freedom. Luis refused to cancel the challenge.

His rival was of different metal, though. Cepeda refused the challenge and was never again so high in party affairs. The Muñoz star was rising, and his rivals were dropping away.

Duels were not uncommon in Puerto Rico's heated politics. A few years later, when Luis Muñoz Rivera was editing *La Democracia*, the straightforward newspaper that he had founded, he published an article that enraged Vicente Balbás Capó, one of the top men in the Conservative party and also one of the best swordsmen in Puerto Rico. Balbás had survived many a duel and was a quick man with a challenge.

He wrote a letter to *La Democracia* challenging any member of its staff to a fight. He didn't care who responded; it was an open challenge.

Luis called upon Dr. José Celso Barbosa, to act as his second. The doctor, an excellent swordsman, was shocked. He was a personal friend of Muñoz, although they had many a difference in party policies.

Dr. Celso Barbosa tried to get Luis to change his mind about the duel, reminding him that Balbás was an "artist" with the sword, while Luis' greatest weapon was the pen.

But Luis was stubborn, insisting that it was a matter of honor. He was editor of the paper and believed he had to take the responsibility himself. He would ask no one to take his place. Luis believed that if he backed down he would become the laughing stock of Puerto Rico. He earnestly wanted Dr. Celso Barbosa to act as his second.

José Celso Barbosa went to see the Conservative duelist, as Luis' second. He was very formal, as called for by the *code duelo*, but his face was very cold.

Dr. Celso Barbosa explained to Señor Balbás that Muñoz had accepted the challenge and would meet Balbás with swords.

Balbás smiled. He seemed to have no doubts about the results. It was well known that Luis Muñoz Rivera had not spent the long hours in sword practice to which his opponent was accustomed.

Dr. Celso Barbosa added coldly that he had had his differences with Don Luis, but nevertheless

still believed that Muñoz was the hope of Puerto Rico. Dr. Celso Barbosa then said that if Don Luis fell in the duel the next day, his own seconds would call on Señor Balbás before the day was out.

The duel took place as scheduled, and it ended with a slight wound taken by Muñoz. Vicente Balbás Capó knew very well that if he had killed the popular editor, he would have had to fight a dozen duels before the week was out.

Things were coming to a head by 1887, and Governor Palacio threw literally hundreds of the Autonomists into jail. Afraid that word of his high-handed tactics would get back to Spain, he forbade anyone to leave the island. However, the patriots managed to smuggle Juan Arrillaga Roque out of the country to Madrid, where he revealed the plight of Puerto Rico. King Alfonso XII replaced the unpopular governor, but the year 1887 is still known in Puerto Rico as "El Año Terrible" (The Terrible Year).

Local politics were so confused at the time that occasionally one member of a family belonged to one party while another belonged to the opposite. In 1889, in the elections for the Provincial Assembly, Luis' father was nominated as the Conservative delegate from Juana Días, and Luis himself was nominated for the same office as an Autonomist. Out of respect for his father, Luis Muñoz Rivera ran instead in the district of Caguas, where he won. The Conservatives challenged him, and, although his election was eventually admitted, the term of his office was by that time already over.

Secret organizations had begun to spring up, and the Autonomists met in the back of Del Valle's drugstore in San Juan to plan their campaigns. The Sociedad Torre del Viejo (Society of the Old Man's Tower) was formed to boycott the businesses of the Conservatives and to support only native-owned Puerto Rican ventures.

Not only was Muñoz accused of belonging to this organization, but the mayor of Barranquitas also charged that he was a leader of the mysterious El Corazón Negro (The Black Heart). Luis could only laugh and pointed out that he didn't even know what the organization believed in, if it existed at all.

On July 1, 1890, he founded his newspaper *La Democracia* (The Democracy) and immediately rose to the heights of his party. The paper was devoted largely to politics, but it also carried poetry and short stories by local writers. Time and again, Luis was criticized by the authorities for going too far.

Before the paper was a year old he was arrested

and transferred to the city of Cayey. Hundreds of protests went up all over Puerto Rico, and the authorities moved him to Guayama, afraid that his followers might attempt to free the youthful editor. It proved too dangerous to hold him, and after three days of arrest Luis was freed when his father posted fifteen thousand pesetas for bond.

His ringing articles were being read by all those who desired Puerto Rican freedom.

In 1891 he wrote:

We pursue a noble and just ideal and we won't conceal it in the shadow. We want to vigorize our people; teach them to love their small piece of America with idolatry; present to them examples of heroism; elevate their spirit very high; create in their bosom a collective valor that will not be confused with individual valor, and to prepare them in this way for any future eventualities.

He had had to sell his interest in his store to raise the money to begin his newspaper in Ponce, and the editor of *El Pueblo,* Ramón Marín, gave him a hand in its beginning. But Ramón Marín gave more than editorial assistance, for Luis was now thirty-four years of age and beginning to think of marriage. In 1893 he married Amalia Marín, daughter of his friend, in the Ponce cathedral.

It was a step he was never to regret. Doña

Amalia was to stand by him through all his battles, through the bad years as well as the good. She was extremely interested in his goals and helped to carry them out long after he had passed away, assisting his son Luis Muñoz Marín when he took up the fight.

Indeed, in March 1941, when the younger Muñoz was president of the Puerto Rican senate and very ill, he named Doña Amalia his political heir in case he died. She was a brave, beautiful, intelligent and well-educated woman.

Puerto Rico was not alone in having difficulties in the 1890's. Spain was also going through a political upheaval, and in Cuba the rebels had taken to the hills and were fighting a guerrilla war against the Spanish troops.

Some extremist Puerto Rican patriots wished to do the same thing in Puerto Rico, and an underground organization was set up in New York City, with open warfare in mind. However, Luis Muñoz Rivera was against it. For one thing, he had no desire to break away completely from Spain; for another he felt violence could never succeed in bringing the home rule for which his people yearned.

Instead, as head of the major faction of the Autonomist party, he sailed to Spain to study the situation there. He soon came to realize that Práxedes

Mateo Sagasta, the long-time head of the Liberal Fusion party in Spain, was the man with whom to identify. He had several times been premier but at this point was out of office.

While Luis was in Madrid, he received the news that his father had died in Barranquitas. Although he and the older Luis often had had many differences in their political beliefs, they had always loved each other as father and son, and the death strongly affected Luis Muñoz. Later, when he returned to Puerto Rico, he was to write about his father in *La Democracia*.

When Muñoz returned to San Juan, he found that his trip to Spain had caused a great controversy. The ranks of the Autonomist party were split. The followers of Dr. José Celso Barbosa, who were called the *Barbosistas,* as opposed to the followers of Muñoz, who were called *Muñocistas,* were against lining up with Sagasta on the grounds that he was a monarchist, and they wanted a republic. Dr. Celso Barbosa had received his education in the United States and was a great admirer of republican institutions.

However, the Autonomists finally agreed to send four men, including Muñoz, to confer with the Liberal Fusion party, and 1896 they sailed for Spain.

They returned with Sagasta's offer. If he became the new premier of Spain, Puerto Rico was to receive a Charter of Autonomy under which she would have equal standing with the provinces of Spain. Although there would still be a Spanish governor, his powers would be limited, and he would be more of an ambassador than a dictator, as in the past.

Dr. Celso Barbosa and his followers were indignant and resigned en masse. They formed their own organization, the Orthodox Autonomist party, and became known as *puros* (purists).

However, when Sagasta won his election, he stuck to his word. Puerto Rico was given her charter in December 1897, and an Executive Council of six men was announced.

Muñoz had changed the name of his group to the Liberal party as he had promised the Spaniards. Now three of these were represented on the Executive Council, including Luis Muñoz Rivera, whose title was Secretary of Grace, Justice and Government. He was thirty-eight years old at the time and the most important man of Puerto Rico. Shortly after, he was made president of the Council of Secretaries and head of the government.

Other matters were at work, however, that would dash all the brave accomplishments of Muñoz and his people, for important changes were taking place in the north on the mainland.

The United States, which had started as thirteen colonies on the Atlantic coast hardly more than a century earlier, had spread across the continent all the way to the Pacific. And voices were heard that she should not stop there. Other powerful countries, such as Great Britain, France and Germany, had colonies all over the world. Did not the United States also have a "Manifest Destiny"? Many influential people thought she did.

Nor was it to be forgotten that in the long Indian wars and especially the Civil War the Americans had built up the strongest army and navy on earth, led by Civil War generals and admirals from both the Union and Confederate sides.

On February 16, 1898, Dr. José Celso Barbosa hurried into the Muñoz office, his face jubilant, a news report clutched in his hand.

He asked Don Luis if he had heard the news that the American battleship *Maine,* which had sailed into Havana harbor in Cuba to look out for American interests there, had been mysteriously blown up and sunk.

Muñoz stared at him in amazement. Such an event would mean war! The Americans would use it as an excuse to declare war on Spain.

Dr. Celso Barbosa believed that the United States would surely liberate Puerto Rico.

But Muñoz was shaking his head sadly. The

Americans had been thinking about building a canal through Panama. If they did it, then they would want Puerto Rico for themselves to help protect the canal.

Dr. Celso Barbosa insisted that this would never happen.

It did happen, however. On May 12, 1898, an American fleet of eight ships pulled off San Juan and began shelling El Morro. The Spanish fought back and at first Muñoz and the Liberal party supported the government of Spain, although many on the island agreed with Dr. Celso Barbosa in thinking the Americans would liberate them completely from the old country.

One shell landed deep in the old fort and blew up a chamber, but El Morro, as so often before, held out.

Muñoz had been correct. The United States, prodded by such aggressive patriots as William Randolph Hearst, who owned a string of influential newspapers from coast to coast, wanted not only Puerto Rico but the Philippine Islands as well.

The Spanish-American War was in many ways a farce. Spain was old and feeble, not the great power she had been four hundred years before. Her fleets were sunk and her armies were destroyed in a matter of months. Indeed, some were afraid that Spain would surrender and that the war would be over before Puerto Rico was captured.

On July 25, 1898, General Nelson Appleton Miles, the Civil War hero and the Indian fighter who had conquered both the Sioux warchief Crazy Horse and Chief Joseph of the Nez Percé tribe, landed at Guánica on the southern coast of Puerto Rico with 3,400 troops.

There was no fight left in the Spanish. The American humorist of the time, Mr. Dooley, called the invasion, "General Miles' Gran' Picnic and Moonlight Excursion in Puerto Rico."

Dr. Celso Barbosa and his *puros* were jubilant and welcomed the newcomers with open arms. They held a meeting and declared that they first expected Puerto Rico to become a territory of the United States and then a state of the Union in the near future.

Luis Muñoz Rivera knew better. The successful war party in America had no intention of making Puerto Rico's people citizens of the United States, not to speak of the island becoming a state. A military government took over. When peace was signed with Spain on August 12, the island was ceded to the United States, as were the Philippines in the Pacific.

Muñoz, who had now seen the end of all his dreams of Puerto Rican self-government, refused to cooperate with the military government and returned to Barranquitas with Doña Amalia and their new child, Luis Muñoz Marín, who had been born in February 1898, on Fortaleza Street in San Juan.

There he took up his pen once again and wrote his most famous poem, "Sísifo" (Sisyphus). In Greek mythology, Sisyphus was the unfortunate man who was supposedly so clever that he even outwitted Pluto, king of the underworld. However, Zeus became angry with Sisyphus and condemned him to eternal punishment in Hades, where each day he was required to push a big rock to the top of a steep hill, only to have it roll down again each evening.

Luis Muñoz Rivera saw this as an example of his own life and of the fate of Puerto Rico. The Puerto Rican people had struggled very hard to push their heavy rock of freedom to the top of the hill, and then at the moment of success, when self-government had been achieved, war had come and the rock had slipped from their grasp and rolled back to the bottom again.

Muñoz was not the type of man who could give up. Any defeat for him was only a temporary defeat.

He returned to San Juan, and when requested by the head of the United States military occupation government, General John R. Brooke, to remain in office with his cabinet, Muñoz accepted.

Shortly after, however, Brooke was replaced by General Guy V. Henry, and sparks began to fly. He was a rugged soldier, and neither he nor Muñoz knew how to pull their punches.

General Henry knew little about Spanish people or their institutions. He had never been in a land with a Spanish background and had little knowledge of the problems of Puerto Rico. He and Luis Muñoz Rivera were continually arguing about almost every aspect of local affairs. Since Muñoz knew only a smattering of English, at best, and General Henry spoke no Spanish at all, they had to conduct their heated debates through an interpreter.

Matters finally came to a head one day when the general snapped to the interpreter that he was sick of hearing Muñoz argue about every decision. The general informed him that on other occasions he had knocked down bigger men than Muñoz.

This was an indication, by the way, that the general had knocked down some very big men in his time, since Muñoz was large and strong.

Muñoz snapped back to the interpreter that if the general wished to behave violently toward him, Muñoz would be obliged to throw him out the window.

So all was not exactly calm on the island of Puerto Rico during the early days of the United States occupation.

5

Victory—and the End

Luis Muñoz Rivera could stand the conflict no longer. In 1899 he resigned his post as president of the Council of Secretaries. Puerto Rico now went through one of the most desperate periods of its history. A great deal of the problem was caused by the inability of the islanders and the mainland Americans to understand each other. They had so very little in common with which to work.

When General Miles had landed with his troops at Guánica, one of the first things he did was to issue a proclamation of friendship for the Puerto Rican people, announcing that the United States did not intend to alter the island's customs and laws. The manner in which Puerto Ricans lived was to remain up to them.

He could hardly have been more wrong. What little independence the Puerto Rican people had obtained from Spain was largely abolished.

Under the self-government granted by Spain, there had been universal suffrage (all adults could vote). But now, under the U.S. military government, only men over twenty-one years of age who were either property owners or who were able to read and write were eligible. Since more than 85 per cent of the Puerto Ricans were illiterate, practically nobody could vote for the officials they wanted to represent them. The population at this time was about one million, but only 51,649 voted in that first election.

On April 12, 1900, President McKinley of the United States signed the Foraker Act, which provided for the ending of the military government and the start of a civil government for Puerto Rico. Senator Joseph B. Foraker of Ohio had written the law, and it took effect on May 1.

It was called the Organic Act, and not a single Puerto Rican had had any say in its writing. Senator Foraker—with all the good will in the world, perhaps—had very little knowledge of the island that his law was to dominate for the next fifteen years and more.

It provided for a Supreme Court of five members, all of them Americans appointed by the President. In Washington, Puerto Rico was to be represented by exactly one elected Resident Commissioner in the House of Representatives, where he could speak but had no vote. The American-appointed governor had the right to cancel any legislation passed on the island, but if any managed to slip by him, by mistake, Congress reserved the right to cancel it, and also reserved the right to legislate for Puerto Rico.

Those who followed Dr. Celso Barbosa hailed the new law as a step in the right direction and changed their name to the Republican party. The Muñocistas who had started up a new newspaper called *El Diario*, edited by Muñoz, changed their name to the Federal party, still demanding more freedom.

As ever, Luis Muñoz Rivera pulled no punches in the columns of *El Diario*, and more than once the tempers of the Republicans flared up at his words. In September 1900, so enraged did some of them become that the followers of Muñoz formed an armed group to act as his bodyguards.

Information got around that there was going to be an attempt to assassinate the editor, and Luis' friends went to his house to meet fire with fire.

Exactly what happened was long debated, but there was yelling and then gunfire at Luis' home. Happily, nobody was killed and the armed strangers escaped.

Now came an indication of how the authorities were taking sides. Muñoz and several of his friends were arrested for armed assault with deadly weapons. Evidently it was thought that they did not have the right to defend themselves! The case against them didn't hold up, of course, and all were turned free.

Each week that went by seemed to bring to the attention of Muñoz some item that was helping to sink his beloved island deeper and deeper into the mud.

One item in the Foraker Act had seemed to be all for the good. It provided that nobody, not even a corporation, would be allowed to own or control more than five hundred acres of land. The act was designed to keep all the farm land from getting into the hands of a few people, thus preventing the native Puerto Ricans, the farmers, from becoming landless.

It was possibly a good law, indeed, but there were no teeth in it, no way of enforcing it. In no time at all, four large American corporations obtained practically all the best land on the fertile coastal plains, by purchase, by rent or by the closing of mortgages.

This situation was to continue until 1940, at which time the Eastern Puerto Rico Sugar Company had a plantation of 54,700 acres, of which they had planted only 20,900 acres. The rest of the company's vast holdings were kept in reserve or used for pasture while landless Puerto Rican farmers looked on.

In the past, Puerto Rico had supplied most of its own food, growing scores of different crops. But now it became a one-crop economy, and food had to be brought in from the United States. The growing of sugar to be shipped to the United States dominated Puerto Rican agriculture.

This created a major problem for the Puerto Rican economy.

The Foraker Act gave Puerto Rico free trade with the United States, but it also included the island within the Coastwise Shipping Laws. American ships with their high union wages were the most expensive in the world, and Puerto Rico was forbidden to use any others.

A situation grew up in which it cost only two cents a bag to ship sugar 10,000 miles all the way from the Philippines to New York, while it cost eighteen cents a bag from Puerto Rico to New York, only 1,300 miles. All the other items that had to be shipped in or out of Puerto Rico were increased drastically by such shipping rates.

There was nothing Muñoz and his friends could do.

It was not that the U.S. authorities were not men of good will. But often when they tried to help the most, they failed the most.

The plan was to "Americanize" the island and to do it as soon as possible.

One day Luis Muñoz Rivera was working on his latest article when an agitated friend entered the office of *El Diario*. The newcomer carried a paper in his hand. He waved it at the editor, asking if Muñoz had seen the latest news story about education. The article reported that all schools through the lower grades were to start conducting their classes in English. Muñoz cried out in amazement, exclaiming that there weren't more than a dozen teachers in Puerto Rico who spoke English well enough to teach in that language. He was sure the American plan would fail.

Once again Luis Muñoz Rivera was correct. The school system soon became a shambles. But it was not until 1930 that President Herbert Hoover appointed Dr. José Padín as Commissioner of Education for Puerto Rico. He changed the teaching system so that, although English was a required subject for all students, the elementary and secondary

schools were taught in Spanish. But even that re-
form was too little and too late. As recently as 1940,
56 per cent of Puerto Rican children—between
350,000 and 400,000 pupils—were not in school.
There were not enough schoolrooms for them.

The Americans simply did not understand
Muñoz. It was up to the Puerto Ricans to bring
the truth home to them. So on he fought, writing
his articles and poems, running in the elections,
speaking to the *jíbaros* out in the countryside. Home
rule! Self-government for Puerto Rico!

The reaction? At first it was far from good.

For instance, U.S. District Judge Peter Hamilton
called Muñoz a "little islander" and an "extremist."
And Hamilton was high in Washington political
circles.

"Puerto Ricans," Hamilton said, "have the Latin
American excitability, and I think America should
go slow in granting them anything like autonomy
[home rule]. Their civilization is not at all like ours
yet."

Later on, he went even further, writing, "The
mixture of black and white in Porto Rico threatens
to create a race of mongrels of no use to anyone, a
race of Spanish American talkers. A governor from
the South, or with knowledge of Southern remedies
for that trouble, could, if a wise man, do much. . . ."

In actuality, Puerto Rico had a proud heritage as far as the relationship between whites and Negroes was concerned. About a quarter of its people were black, a quarter mulatto and the remainder white. Long since, they had come to live together with little prejudice. Indeed, Román Baldorioty de Castro, the early inspiration of Luis Muñoz Rivera, had a mulatto mother. And Dr. José Celso Barbosa, the life-long friend, though political rival, of Muñoz was a Negro.

Puerto Rico's problems were growing rapidly, and even Luis Muñoz Rivera was sometimes on the edge of despair.

The population was growing fantastically as modern medicine cut the death rate. Even today Puerto Rico is one of the most densely populated areas in the world. The density of population in the United States proper is less than 50 persons per square mile, while in Puerto Rico it is 682 per square mile. Only Java in the South Pacific has a greater density.

Thus, with the new one-crop economy—sugar—large numbers of people could find work only during the few months of the cutting and grinding. Pay was as little as forty cents a day, and prices for necessary things, shipped in from the United States, were higher than they were on the mainland.

Poverty stalked the land.

As late as 1941, when the American journalist John Gunther published his book *Inside Latin America,* his vivid report on Puerto Rico was shocking. He claimed that the villages he saw there were dirtier than anything in the most squalid parts of China; that Puerto Rican children, living in hovels worse than anything he had seen in Calcutta, India, were starving and ridden by disease.

Gunther discovered that in some of the villages 100 per cent of the people had malaria, and that infant deaths were four times as high as in the United States proper—giving Puerto Rico the highest infant mortality in the world. And still, at that late date, the average income of the *jíbaro* was only $135 a year. In modern America a skilled workingman expects that much a week.

Gunther pointed out fact after fact to illustrate Puerto Rican poverty, including that while Americans drank three-quarters of a pint of milk a day, the Puerto Ricans averaged only one teaspoon a day. And even that small amount of milk was unfit to drink because of unsanitary conditions. Not even the public water supply could be trusted.

Long before this report, which shocked the United States, Luis Muñoz Rivera had realized that if his people were ever going to achieve their needs the struggle would have to be taken to the mainland. Since he could think of no one else to do it, he would have to take the step himself.

He had moved to the town of Caguas and re-opened his original paper, *La Democracia.* He felt that it was not the Puerto Ricans that had to be made aware of the situation—they knew it very well already. Rather it was the United States that had to be told the story.

He turned over the editing of the paper to one of his followers, and in 1901, together with Doña Amalia and their three-year-old son Luisito ("little Luis"), he boarded a ship for New York City.

Already there were quite a few Puerto Ricans living in that great city. Most of them had come looking for work, since there were so few jobs on their island home. And most of them, Muñoz was to find, hated it in New York. They missed the quiet Spanish-type towns of Puerto Rico, the tropical food with which they were so familiar, the soft Spanish language and the almost perfect climate of which Puerto Rico boasts.

Luis Muñoz Rivera and Doña Amalia also missed Puerto Rico. Luisito, being so young, adapted and was soon speaking much better English than either his mother or father. Indeed, he picked up the language with a heavy New York accent, which later in life he had to strive to un-learn.

However, the Muñoz family had not come to the most important city in the United States with the intention of merely enjoying it. They had come to work, and Muñoz soon opened the *Puerto Rico Herald.*

He wrote the articles in Spanish for the new crusading newspaper, but then had assistants translate them into English so that the publication could be in both languages.

His attacks upon what was being done to Puerto Rico were forceful and direct. He wrote:

> We affirm the right of Puerto Rico to assert its own personality, either through Statehood or independence. If the United States continues to humiliate and shame us, we can forget about Statehood and support independence, with or without U.S. protection. In 1901 only a few of us distrusted the United States. Today, all are beginning to realize that we have been deceived. We no longer worship everything that comes from the North.

Strong words indeed, but there was much more of the same.

After years in New York, the Muñoz family finally returned to the island. Little Luisito, now eight years old, was put into a private school in San Juan. His father immediately slipped back into local politics and was twice elected to the Chamber of Delegates.

However, it was still his opinion that the big fight must be fought in the United States, and in 1910 Luis Muñoz Rivera campaigned for the office of Resident Commissioner. While he was in New York, the Federal party had changed its name to the Unión de Puerto Rico (the Unionist party), and now under its banner he received more than 100,000 votes, while the largest of the opposition parties, the Republicans, was able to get only 59,000.

Resident Commissioner was the highest possible office for a Puerto Rican to hold, and Luis Muñoz Rivera kept the job from 1910 to 1916, when his health failed. He was only fifty-one when elected and was to spend the balance of his life at it. Already he had been striving for twenty years, but the end was not yet in sight.

His first task was to learn English well. He certainly was not going to be able to speak in Congress, to discuss Puerto Rican affairs with senators, representatives, cabinet members and even the President in his own language. He spent more than a full year at this, and at the age of fifty-one it was not an easy job.

From the first he began to make some friends among the politicians in Washington who realized the sincerity and energetic efforts of the fiery Puerto Rican.

Henry L. Stimpson was one of them and appeared before the Senate in 1912 to urge citizenship for Puerto Rico. He said:

Last summer I traveled through the West Indies and saw a good many Latin-American peoples, and I found that when they would speak to me frankly they regarded this attitude of the United States toward Puerto Rico as an evidence that we regarded not only the people there, but Latin-American people in general, as of a different class from ourselves, and of an inferior class. And therefore not only in respect to our political relations with Puerto Rico itself, but to our diplomatic relations with other countries of the same blood, it seems to be a very deep-seated sore and irritation.

Felix Frankfurter, later to become a United States Supreme Court Justice, also supported Muñoz, saying:

There is nothing in the Constitution to hamper the responsibility of Congress in working out, step by step, forms of government for our insular possessions (such as Puerto Rico) responsive to the largest needs and capacities of their inhabitants.

Only a small number of men in Washington, however, really cared about Puerto Rico. The island had no lobby except one proud, imposing, solitary man struggling forcefully with his English grammar, doing his best to understand Congressional mentality, and always thinking of his party and his homeland.

It was a lonesome life and continued to grow depressing to him. To a friend in Puerto Rico who had written to him complaining about political troubles on the island, Muñoz wrote:

But you are there, surrounded by your friends and associates, and by a host of people who know you and speak your language, and grasp what you say and are either your friends or your enemies. But I am here alone, in a tomb-like isolation, mixing with people who speak a different tongue, who have no affinity with my way of life, who are not even hostile . . . but indifferent, cold, and rough as the granite stones which support their big Capitol. Compare and understand that you live in the best of possible worlds.

Nevertheless, progress was being made. In January 1916, Congressman William A. Jones, a Virginia Democrat, prepared what the Puerto Ricans promptly named "El Bill Jones." It proved to be the first big breakthrough, since it provided that Puerto Ricans could become full United States citizens. They would be able to come and go freely within the United States and were protected by American laws, while still not having to contribute to the Federal treasury.

The bill was presented on January 20, and im-

mediately Muñoz went to work fighting for it. He made a ringing speech in excellent English before the House of Representatives on May 5, 1916, and was even given a private audience with President Woodrow Wilson, who proved to be sympathetic.

However, the long years of fighting for Puerto Rican rights had proved a great strain on the health of Luis Muñoz Rivera. He had been working under too great a pressure. In hopes of regaining his strength, in September 1916 he returned to his beloved island, very ill. He died in his village of Barranquitas at the age of only fifty-seven, surrounded by a multitude of followers. All Puerto Rico mourned. Muñoz passed away only a few months before some of his fondest dreams were to be realized.

The following year, on March 2, President Wilson signed the Jones Bill, and it became law. Puerto Rico still had a long way to go to achieve her present comparative well-being and prosperity, but Luis Muñoz Rivera had cleared the way.

The stone over his grave is very simple. It reads, *Luis Muñoz Rivera, 1859–1916.* But nothing more is needed. Every Puerto Rican knows what he did.

Every American should feel proud of him.

6

Like Father, Like Son

The first big battle for home rule, national respect and eventual prosperity had been won. But there were other struggles yet to be made into victories.

Luis Muñoz Rivera had fallen under the burden. Many of the old hands who had nursed the flower of Puerto Rican freedom were gone. Old Román Baldorioty de Castro had died as far back as September 30, 1889. The fiery poet José de Diego was to pass away on July 16, 1918, and Dr. José Celso

Barbosa not long afterward on September 21, 1921.

New hands had to be found to take up the torch of freedom and prosperity.

They were found, not surprisingly perhaps, in Luis Muñoz Marín, young Luisito, who had grown up in the atmosphere of Puerto Rico's struggles. He, like his father before him, was to spend his adult life working for Puerto Rico, and, unlike his father, was to see the final triumph.

Luisito had been eight years of age when his family returned from New York to Puerto Rico the first time. His father had enrolled him in Don Pedro Moczó's private school in San Juan, and he attended it for four years, an outstanding scholar.

When Muñoz Rivera returned to Washington, Luisito, as they still called him, was soon enrolled in Georgetown University and spent three years there, although he never took a degree, since his education was interrupted by his father's untimely death.

He had returned with the family to Puerto Rico in 1916, and following his father's funeral services, at the age of eighteen, he took his mother to San Juan and saw her settled where she could live on a small income from *La Democracia*. An indication of the honesty of Luis Muñoz Rivera can be seen in the fact that he left only four hundred dollars to his heirs. He had obviously not used his political positions to enrich himself.

Luis Muñoz Marín now had to make his own way. He returned to the United States as secretary to the new Resident Commissioner who had taken over his father's position in Washington.

Somehow, what had been in his father's blood was transmitted to him. He wanted to write, and especially, at first, poetry. Within the year he had published two books, *Madre Haraposa* (Mother in Rags) and *Borrones* (Sketches). Both of these were in Spanish, although he also could and did write in English.

Washington is the political center of the United States, however, not its literary and publishing center. In 1918 Muñoz Marín moved to New York City and to the section of town where the artists and writers gathered—Greenwich Village.

It was here, in 1919, that he met the American poetess Muna Lee, while he was editor of *La Revista de Indies* (The Review of the Indies). They were married on July 1, and later two children were born to them, Muna in 1920 and Luis in 1921. Unhappily, the marriage failed to work out, and they separated. Later he married a second wife, Inés Mendoza, and they had two girls, Viviana and Victoria.

For a time Muñoz Marín tried to interest himself in mainland politics and campaigned for the liberal La Follette in 1924, but even then his heart was probably back in Puerto Rico. By 1926 he had returned and was occupying his father's former chair as editor of *La Democracia*. And, of course, he immediately became active in his father's party.

Although Puerto Ricans were now United States citizens, the old problem of poverty was still with them, and the big sugar companies of the north still dominated their island. Muñoz Marín at first came to the opinion that the only answer was to become independent.

The world depression was in full swing by the thirties, and three out of five Puerto Ricans were out of work. Obviously, some important changes had to be made.

In July 1938 Muñoz Marín formed a new party, the Popular Democratic party, and a strong platform was presented to the people.

There were many difficult times, with both successes and failures. The Popular Democratic party finally came to power in 1940. In 1947 a new law was passed by the U.S. Congress that in the Puerto Rican election of 1948, and from then on, the governor of Puerto Rico was to be elected by the island's voters.

Needless to say, it was Luis Muñoz Marín who became the first Puerto Rican to be elected governor. The Puerto Rican people were to re-elect him three times and would have elected him again, had he not refused because of advancing age.

Under Muñoz Marín and his followers, Puerto Rico boomed. The new government acted under the federal "Five-Hundred Acre Law" and set out, as fast as funds were made available, to take over some of the lands held by the big corporations. These were turned over to the farmers.

Above all was "Operation Bootstrap," a plan to industrialize the island. Muñoz realized that though Puerto Rico was poor in minerals and other resources, so were other countries such as Switzerland, the Netherlands and Denmark, all of which were very prosperous. If those countries could do it, so could Puerto Rico.

Industrialists were urged to come to the island and were offered freedom from taxes for prolonged periods. It was pointed out to them that labor was cheap in Puerto Rico, and since the island was part of the United States there was a ready market up north for anything produced.

Industry boomed and so did tourism. By the end of Muñoz Marín's fourth term in office, more than a thousand factories had gone up, providing more than 70,000 jobs. In 1940 the average yearly income had been only $120. By 1965 it was up to $830 for every man, woman and child on the island, and by 1966 it had gone over the $900 mark.

Today, the per capita income of Puerto Ricans is over $1,000, the highest in Latin America, though still far below the mainland United States. As a comparison, that of progressive Japan was only $857 as of 1965 and that of neighboring Mexico only $455.

This was not all.

In 1950 Congress passed a new law allowing Puerto Rico to write its own constitution and organize a new government after its own desires. And on July 25, 1952, the Commonwealth of Puerto Rico was proclaimed. Although still associated with the United States, and *part* of the United States, the island of Puerto Rico is now self governing. If she chooses, she can sever what lines still remain and be completely independent, but most Puerto Ricans do not wish this.

It had been a long, long struggle, first by the father, then by the son, but Luis Muñoz Marín was right when he said, "What counts is what a country *wants* to be. The goal is the important thing. If a country wishes to be a democracy, it should be treated like one."

Index

Index